BURY ME IN THE BACKYARD

FILLING THE GRAVE OF MY FATHER

Brittany Yenser

Presentation by *BookLeaf Publishing*

Web: www.bookleafpub.com

E-mail: info@bookleafpub.com

ISBN: 9789358738650

First edition 2021

ACKNOWLEDGEMENT

I would like to thank Alyssa Meadows, who is one of the most amazing women I know. She encourages me to be more than I think I can be. Without her, I would have never known about this opportunity, nor would I have had the courage to pursue it.

I would also like to thank James Zengerle, who, in college, told me my poetry reminded him of E.E. Cummings. James—that compliment, that you probably don't even remember, encouraged me to keep writing.

And last but certainly not least, I would like to thank Kashi Johnson. Ms. Johnson took me, a random and timid college kid, and put me on a stage where I shared my poetry for the first time. That was a life changing opportunity, and I am forever grateful.

PREFACE

I grew up in a rural area with two parents, who, like most parents, were doing their best while battling their own demons. My father's death created a canyon in our lives, and I allowed my pain to echo for far too long. Through these poems, I explored my feelings from the initial loss, the long loop of the grieving process, and finally, the freedom of "the other side" of grief. It is my greatest hope that these poems reach someone who is also experiencing the "grief journey." Please believe me when I say: it does, for real, get better—if you let it.

DEDICATION

These works are dedicated to my parents, John Anthony and Elizabeth Wilczewski, who both laid the foundation for the woman I have become.

I would also like to dedicate this work to my husband, Chase Yenser, who dares me to dream in ways I never did before.

1. BUT LATER NEVER CAME

My mind keeps flashing
to our unknowing goodbye.
"Do you want to go for a ride?"
"No--
I'll stay home."
The summer sun was shining
on your face
as you stood in the open doorway.
I could smell cleaning products
in the next room,
and I could feel my agitation
rising.
Over the sound of the vacuum,
"Are you sure?"
"Yeah,"
a beat
I'll stay home."
"Okay, I'll see you later."
The creak of the screen door
punctuating
a normal exchange.

2. THREE WISHES

I remember wishing you would leave,
if only for a little while—
wishing for a lag in the yelling,
the slamming of cabinets
and doors,
the distinctive sound of a beer can being opened.
Crack. Fizz. Silence.

I remember the deafening silence
as I sat staring at your empty seat,
wondering when you would return.

I remember knowing change was imminent
when, astounded by the nurse's bedside manner,
she told me you were not alright and
speeding was not encouraged but it was
advised.

I remember wishing you could come back,
if only for a little while--

For years I'd wished for things to change,
and now I wish I would have understood
that wishing can make you bitter,
silent—
lost in remembering.

3. IT'S A BAD HABIT

Cut to
Old Milwaukee in a cold glass mug
on a hot summer day--
a crisp, yellow color and a
bitter-sweet scent.
White froth hit his mouth and he
flipped something on the grill.
"Go get me a pack of cigarettes…
please."
I always liked to open them, and
sometimes I dreamt of their
hazy taste.
But as he lit up this time
he told me he wasn't
afraid
of dying.
He breathed deep,
exhaled his life,
and I still wonder what it tasted like.

4. SCATTERED

Ashes blowing in the wind--
a sign of no remorse and
rash reactions.
The energy has changed
twice over.
The house where we'd lived now
cold. Alive.
The very walls breathing
a sigh of relief.
The emptiness strangely
soothing--
familiar, irrational,
final.

5. FORCED PERSPECTIVE

I find myself crawling
into the cold, dark earth--
buried in a moist fog
as cleansing rain packs the dirt.

I find myself riding the wind--
gusting air penetrating
every layer of my being and
whisking me through the sky.

I find myself floating
over beautiful landscapes--
scattered over fields of swaying grass,
over dense forests and over
snowcapped mountains.

I find myself carried
away
from the places I used to know.

I find myself feeling
free.

And I find myself hoping
as I touch down in a flowing stream
that the feeling
is mutual.

6. REFLECTIONS

There are cracks in the walls of this old house,
where memories have seeped inside.
In one, I'm running through
dew covered grass
while you drink black coffee and
smoke a cigarette pulled from a
red and white pack.
By now the smell of smoke has faded and
memories like this one keep
slipping through the cracks.

I often find myself sitting in that
same grass,
cut too short,
sun dried and
full of weeds,
wondering what you'd think of me.
'Cause I'm still as unsure as that girl you knew
and I still can't pronounce 'Marlboros.'

Maybe it's best we don't
know each other now--
just one more thought to
nestle into this place we'd made home.

Just a thought.

7. THE FIRST REPLACEMENT

Lost lingerie and
a new tube of red lipstick.
Her cries of passion are
a mimicry of something
sinister.

8. ALONE TOGETHER

Give me one more interruption,
a ringing phone or a
knock on the bolted door.
I can feel our feelings gather,
and crash as the tide does to the shore.
And I can feel us drifting,
"We" is slowly morphing into
"I".
We should have been prepared for this,
I,
I should have known.

9. AN EXIT STRATEGY

A point of desperation,
pandora's box opened.
A flickering thought,
and then
nothing.

10. BUT NEVER LATER CAME, REPRISED

Every day, the same image,
playing in my mind like a
movie reel.
Sometimes, it flickers,
cigarette burns.
But always the same scene
with the same ending and
the same suffering,
replaying.

11. HAVE YOU TRIED TALKING ABOUT IT?

Reaching out,
every now and then.
casually asking
to be saved.
No one feels like being
a hero today.
Music blasts somewhere and
the smell of alcohol
permeates the hall.
I feel alone, but
it seems everyone else feels
fine.
I stop reaching,
reclusive.

12. DON'T LEAVE ME HANGING (ON THE TELEPHONE)

I've realized the rest of my life
is a long time--
I can't quite recall
what your voice sounds like,
and we'll never have another
conversation.
She says I was your world once and maybe
that's true.
I didn't always feel it, and
you
couldn't always show it.
But I don't blame you anymore.
I wish I could say more
to you now than
a few uttered prayers,
the way we talk to
invisible fathers.
I hope I'll hear your voice again
when I
get called Home.

13. DAY DREAMING

I find myself
slipping
in and out of realities.
Some fantasies are
dangerously appealing,
and I feel myself drifting
further with each thought.
I wonder
if I could stay in a world of
my own creation,
how quickly I would choose
to
abandon everything.

14. HAVE YOUR TRIED ASKING REDDIT?

Something isn't right.
The way we speak
and when—
roles reversed.
He isn't here to
take the blame and now
you say I'm just like
Him.
I wish I had the answers
but sometimes
I don't understand the question.
I've heard there are forums
for this
but
I don't know if I should use them.

15. THINKING ABOUT GROWING UP

I've got a nostalgia
that
appeals to the senses.
A childhood that
smells like cigarette smoke
and has the faint image of
a ring-shaped stain
from a beer mug.
Looking back, everything
tastes like a secret recipe
and feels like
frustration.
In my memories, all I can hear is
laughter.
Now, living
a bitter numbness, I
fear I'm just a shell
of what I used to be.

16. LOCKED AWAY IN THE TOWER OF GUILT

My problem,
I've found,
stems from the chaos
of grey areas.
He was never quite my
gallant knight, nor
the fearsome dragon
of lore.
And before I could
understand
that he didn't have
to be either/or,
he'd grown tired
of the battle and
slayed them both.

17. AN ALMOST BAPTISM

The air is warm, but
the rain chills my
skin with each
large drop,
raising the hair on
my arms—
seeping into my
pores.
I often wonder
what it's like
for him,
each summer storm
packing his
ashes like
mud.

18. WHILE THE WOMEN COME AND GO

Her voice sounds like sugar
and her breath is laced
with smoke.
Her hands wrap around
an old coffee mug--
steaming.
"I think if I've measured my life
in anything,"
she says
"It's been darkness—
you'll understand
one day."

19. LOST

The sun is hot,
but the air is crisp and
cold.
My lungs stinging,
I've got nowhere else
to go.
He said I would learn
to resent her but
I gave up
years ago.
Now, the winter air
intoxicating,
I feel
alone.

20. HAVE YOU TRIED THERAPY?

What if this sadness
is who I am now?
Do I have a
personality
outside of this
perpetual grief?
If I get help,
who will I
become?

21. THERE'S SOMETHING ROMANTIC ABOUT DRIVING WITH THE LOW FUEL LIGHT ON

I'm often asked
why
the floor of
my car is so
littered
with junk.
I'll never admit
that I
almost live
in that old
dented ford—
constantly in motion.
I'm drifting
through snow,
I blink, and
suddenly the
trees are lush
and green
again.
I'm running on
empty, but
the key never
seems to leave
the ignition.

22. OUR MONTH

There's nothing like cold October rain
hitting bare skin,
glistening.
It gets colder as the day fades,
the full moon shines
through the fog and
the air is bracing.
I tip toe through
falling leaves--
wet,
and wonder
why.

23. CUT TO: THE COUNTRYSIDE, MIDNIGHT

Sitting on the back deck,
drinking coffee and
longing for a cigarette.
The full moon swallows
the black sky,
and I wonder if he
sees that too.
Maybe now he
sees a different
moon—
or a moonless sky,
lit by the glare of
a million stars.
Or, maybe,
a black void—
nothingness.
I watch an owl swoon
and wonder what
that must be like.

24. ONE, TWO, THREE, FOUR

As I make my way through the cold
winter night,
I count the straggling pennies
in my jacket pocket.
My fingers find each one—
each
smooth, sacred surface.
I search the ground for more—
wondering if he's conscious
and thinking of me.

25. PENNIES FROM HEAVEN

It was another cold
winter day.
I hurried toward the warmth of
my dorm room,
and saw a penny on the sidewalk
glistening from the light of the
midday sun.
I hurried on,
not wanting to stop to claim the
cheap coin.
I passed this same penny again,
and again and
again.
Each time, its color faded,
the sun's light
dimming.
Finally, as night fell and I walked to
my building for the
last time,
I stooped to pick the penny up.
It was cold, even
in my numbing hand, and
I wondered how it went the whole day
unnoticed.
Truly, I thought,
it was a sign he had
meant it for me.
I kept it in my pocket for days,
its smooth surface

reassuring.
When I tired of touching it
every time I sought the warmth
of my pocket,
I dropped it in my
coin jar.
Now, lost amongst other coins
just as special as itself,
it waits to be
cashed in for
something
trivial.

26. MELANCHOLIA

Driving with the window rolled
down
in January--
eyes scanning the road.
Checking the mirrors.
Counting the space between
this car and
the next--
one Mississippi
two Mississippi.
Trying to stay focused--
the mind wanders.
Fingers tap the car door,
the rhythm of an
old song.
It ends as
the car stops--
perfect timing.
Staring straight
ahead, pulling the keys
from the ignition and
listening as it cools down--
ticking, rattling.
Studying the keys in hand--
the thought,
"How did I get here?"

27. IT'S BEEN A JOURNEY

I drop a pin
in my mental map—
keeping track of where
I've been and where
I am
now.
I might not know
where I want to go
next,
but I do know
I'm ready to
get there.

28. THE SEVEN STAGES OF GRIEF

One:
It can't be true—
any day now
I'll come home
from school and
he'll be sitting in his chair,
waiting.

Two:
Maybe—
I should have been
more kind.
More aware.
Maybe—
this is my fault
somehow.

Three:
Desperation—
I would give anything
to say
I'm sorry
for how things
were.

Four:
A deep depression—
I don't deserve
to live in a world

he is no longer
a part of.
Sometimes
I pray I won't
wake up.

Five:
Maybe—
it was not my fault.
A child wearing
grown up shoes
became
a grown up laden
with trauma

Six:
Too many skeletons—
I cannot allow them
to gather more dust
in my closet.
Now—
my therapist says
I am getting better.

Seven:
A new dawn—
I might wake up
tired,
but I am so glad
I wake up.

29. KINTSUKUROI

There is an art of repair
called
kintsukuroi—
broken pieces
of pottery are restored
with gold,
creating beauty
in the cracks.
Something once
shattered,
made whole.
What could have been
discarded
so easily,
made new
instead.
I have found
with a little bit of
time,
love,
and artistry,
people, like pottery,
can be mended and made
new.

30. A EULOGY

When my dad died
we didn't have a funeral.
I wouldn't have had
the words
if we had.
Only after years
of reflection,
heartache,
and renewal
have I learned—
because of him,
I have
my sense of humor
and
commitment to servitude.
I have
my love of books, music and
gardens
and my penchant
for true crime.
In spite of him,
I have a cat
and a huge dog
and I learned
to open my heart to love,
real love,
when it found me.
And so
I would like to close this collection

with gratitude
and joy,
knowing our connection endures,
in spite of ourselves.

9 789358 738650